Do You Know the Meaning of These United States?

by

James Dean

RoseDog Books
PITTSBURGH, PENNSYLVANIA 15238

RoseDog Books
585 Alpha Drive, Suite 103
Pittsburgh, PA 15238
Visit our website at *www.rosedogbookstore.com*

ISBN: 979-8-89027-217-1
eISBN: 979-8-89027-715-2

Do you know the meaning of these United States?

by James Dean

Thank you,

For showing interest in our Country, in the following pages I will be telling you how each state got its name. Some states may surprise you but it is part of the History and legacy of these United States.

At the End of this book is information about the Flag of the United States of America also a crossword puzzle that some historians may struggle to answer, and The Bill of Rights.

<u>The state of Alabama</u> —goes back to the journals of the Spanish explorer Hernando De Soto (1500-1542) Spelled "Alibamu," "Alibamo", The early explorers named the river after an indian tribe that lived in the territory "Alabama.

<u>The state of Alaska</u> = Alaska is taken from the Aleut word "alaxsxag" that refers to an object to which the sea is directed. The United States used this name first to refer to the entire territory and then to the state, after its purchase in 1867.

<u>The state of Arizona</u> —name originated from early spanish name "Arizonoc" from the o'odam name Alisonak meaning "small spring" applied only to an area near the silver mining camp of Plancho de Plata Sonora.

<u>The state of Arkansas</u> = phonetic spelling of the Illinois tribes name for the Quapaw people who lived down river, from either Spanish or french explorers.

<u>The state of California</u> —Named after a romance novel in California is described an island, east of island mainland ruled by Queen Califia and populated only by Amazonian women weilding,

gold weapons. The author of the novel was an early 16th century. Garcia Rodriguez de Mon Talro called Las Sergas Esplandian.

 - The native people called the mohegans who spoke Algonquin. They originally named the river quinituKqut which means long river place.

 - the Colorado river has a reddish hue carrying silt from the mountains. The name "Colorado" is Spanish meaning colored red.

 - named after govenor of Virginia Thomas West, Lord De La Warr by Samuel Argall in 1610 after naming the river and bay "Deleware".

 - is a Spanish word meaning Flowery, covered with flowers. Named by Pince de Leon.

 - named after King George II of England after he granted the states charter in 1732.

 - King Kamehameha I united the islands under his rule by 1819 as the Kingdom of Hawaii.

 - from the Shoshone language "meaning Sun comes from the mountains. George M. Willing suggested the name early 1860's.

The state of Illinois — French Spelling for Illinois and Peoria indian word "illinok" meaning men and warriors. The river name was by French explorer Robert Cavelier Sieur de La Salle in 1679.

The state of Indiana — The United States Congress in 1800 passed legislation to divide the Northwest Territory into two areas then named the western part Indiana, Territory, Indiana means Indian land.

The State of Iowa — The River and State named after the Iowa indians who lived there.

The State of Kansas — From the Kansa indian Tribe

The State of Kentucky — has many different native American language meanings

The State of Louisiana — Named by France after King Louis XIV 1643.

The State of Maine — There is not a clear answer for the name of the state. Could be a "nautical term" or a place in France or England.

Henrietta Maria Lord Baltimore recieved charter from King Charles, what the new colony was to be named after his "Queen Mary."
Not clear if indians or New Englanders named the state.
means "clearing" from the Chippewa indians. Europeans named it in the 1670's.
Siox Indian word Minni - water Sota - cloudy named after the river.
name given by Chippewa Indians means "large River."
from the Siox Tribe Missouria named after the river.
Given by the Spanish explorers from latin word Montanea defined "mountain."
old oto indian word Nebra meaning "flat water."
Spanish word meaning snow covered, from the Sierra Nevada mountain Range.
named after Hampshire, England by Captain John Mason.

The State of New Jersey - Named after an island in the English Channel by Sir George Carteret and Sir John Berkley.

The State of New Mexico - Spaniards called the land to the North and West of Mexico, New Mexico.

The State of New York - named after King James II of England, was Duke of York.

The State of North Carolina - Latin word from Carolus means Charles in honor of Charles IV of France in 1729.

The State of North Dakota - named from the Siox word Dakota meaning "Friends."

The State of Ohio - Seneca Tribe word meaning "Great River" or "large creek."

The State of Oklahoma - Choctaw Tribe meaning native American people as a whole.

The State of Oregon - The name is not clear where it comes from maybe French Canadian.

The State of Pennsylvania - William Penn named it after his father that was persecuted in England for his Quaker faith.

The State of Rhode Island - Named by Giovanni da Verrazzano, explorer 1524 likened the island to the island of Rhodes in the Aegean Sea.

The State of South Carolina - Lation Word from Carolus means Charles in honor of Charles IV of France in 1729.

The State of South Dakota - Same as North, named from the Siox tribe meaning "Friends."

The State of Tennessee - CapT. Juan Pardo Spanish explorer recorded the name in 1567, while traveling in and from South Carolina. As they passed an indian village named "Tanasqui."

The State of Texas - indian word "Tejas" meaning "friends" from Caddo and Hasinais.

The State of Utah - from the native Tribe Nuutsiu or Utes, Utah means "Land of the Sun".

The State of Vermont - Samuel D. Champlain French explorer named them in 1647, called them "Verd Mont" means "green MT."

The state of Virginia - named after Elizabeth I the Virgin Queen.

The state of Washington - Settlers split from Oregon and Congress named it Washington after George Washington.

The state of West Virginia - Almost named after a native tribe river - "Kanawha." In 1862 name changed to West Virginia.

The state of Wisconsin - not clear how the name came about - came from the Algongin word.

The state of Wyoming - comes from the Dakota word "insche wea miing" meaning "at the big flats" or large plains.

Our Constitution Crossword Puzzle of the Fathers:

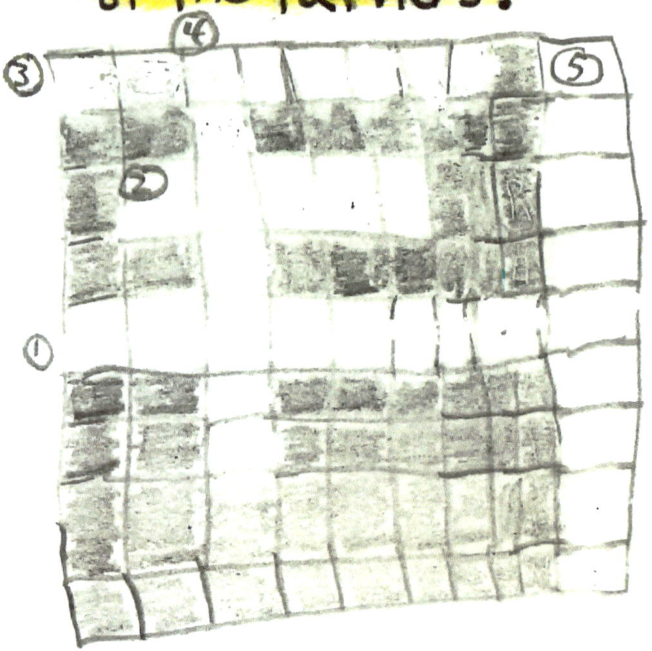

Across

1. Who was the U.S. 1ST president?
2. Who was the U.S. 1ST vice president?
3. Who was the U.S. 1ST Sec. of Treasury?

Down

4. one of the fathers of the Constitution - 4th president
5. only Father to sign all 3 documents Freeing America from Britain: He was Scientist, inventor, politician, Philanthropist and businessman

 —originated
in the Battlefields, as for
identifacation and hiearchy.

The 50 white stars represent
the 50 states of the Union. The
13 red and White stripes represent
the first 13 colonies. The Red,
White and Blue colors stand
as this; White-represents
purity and innocence; Blue-represents
Vigilence, perseverance and justice,
; Red represents Hardiness+Valor.

④
③ H A M I L T O N
A
② A D A M S
D
I
① W A S H I N G T O N
S
O
N
⑤ F R A N K L I N

ANSWERS:

Across
① Washington
② Adams
③ Hamilton

Down
④ Madison
⑤ Franklin

The United STaTes Bill of Rights Comprises the firsT ten amendments To the United STates Constitution: We will Leave you space for Defining each RighT:

① Congress shall maKe no law respecting an establishment of religion or prohibiting the free exercise thereof or abridging the freedom of speech or of the press, or the right of the people peaceably to assemble, and to petition the government for a redress of grievances.

②A well regulated militia, being necessary to the security of a free state, the right of the people to keep and bear Arms, shall not be infringed.—

③ No Soldier shall, in time of peace be quartered in any house, without the consent of the Owner, nor in time of war, but in a manner to be perscribed by law.—

(4) The right of the people, to be
secure in thier persons, houses, papers,
and effects against unreasonable
searches and seizures shall not be
violated, and no warrants shall issue but
upon probable cause, supported by oath
or affirmation and particularly decribing
the place to be searched and the persons
or things to be siezed. —

⑤ No person shall be held to answer for a capital or otherwise infamous crime unless on a presentment or indictment of a grand jury except in cases arising in the land or naval forces, or in the militia, when in actual service in time of war or public danger; nor shall any person be subject for the same offense to be twice put in jeopardy of life or limb; nor shall be compelled in any criminal case to be a witness against himself, nor be deprived of life, liberty, or property without due process of law; nor shall private property be taken for public use without just compensation. —

⑥ In all criminal prosecutions the accused shall enjoy the right to a speedy and public trial by an impartial jury of the state and district wherein the crime shall have been committed, which district shall have been previously ascertained by law, and to be informed of the nature and cause of the accusation: to be confronted with the witnesses against him: to have compulsory process for obtaining witnesses in his favor: and to have the assistance of counsel for his defense.—

⑦ In suits at common law, where the value in controversy shall exceed twenty dollars, the right of trial by jury shall be preserved, and no fact tried by a jury shall be otherwise re examined in any court of the United States than according to the rules of the common law. —

⑧ Excessive bail shall not be required, nor excessive fines imposed nor cruel and unusual punishments inflicted. —

9) The enumeration in the Constitution of certain rights shall not be construed to deny or disparage others retained by the people. —

10) The powers not delegated to the United States by the Constitution, nor prohibited by it to the states, are reserved to the states respectively or to the people. —

www.ingramcontent.com/pod-product-compliance
Lightning Source LLC
Chambersburg PA
CBHW040904110726
48005CB00001B/192